LITTLE W
OF INSPIRA

Friends

© 2009 by Barbour Publishing, Inc.

ISBN 978-1-60260-471-1

Compiled by Amber James.

Scripture quotations marked KJV are taken from the King James Version of the Bible.

Scripture quotations marked NIV are taken from the HOLY BIBLE, NEW INTERNATIONAL VERSION®. NIV®. Copyright © 1973, 1978, 1984 by International Bible Society. Used by permission of Zondervan. All rights reserved.

Scripture quotations marked NLT are taken from the *Holy Bible*, New Living Translation, copyright © 1996, 2004. Used by permission of Tyndale House Publishers, Inc. Wheaton, Illinois 60189, U.S.A. All rights reserved.

Scripture quotations marked CEV are from the Contemporary English Version, Copyright © 1991, 1992, 1995 by American Bible Society. Used by permission.

Published by Barbour Publishing, Inc., P.O. Box 719, Uhrichsville, Ohio 44683, www.barbourbooks.com

Our mission is to publish and distribute inspirational products offering exceptional value and biblical encouragement to the masses.

Member of the
Evangelical Christian
Publishers Association

Printed in China.

LITTLE WHISPERS
OF INSPIRATION FOR
Friends

BARBOUR
PUBLISHING

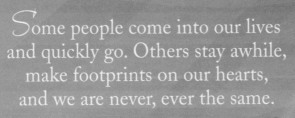

Some people come into our lives
and quickly go. Others stay awhile,
make footprints on our hearts,
and we are never, ever the same.

UNKNOWN

True friends can bring us
happiness with a simple smile.

A friend loveth at all times.

PROVERBS 17:17 KJV

$\mathcal{W}$hat is a friend?
I will tell you. . .it is someone with
whom you dare to be yourself.

FRANK CRANE

Friends are there for one another—
through the good and the bad.

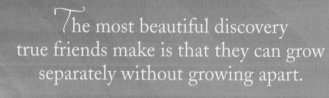

The most beautiful discovery
true friends make is that they can grow
separately without growing apart.

ELIZABETH FOLEY

Laughter shared among friends brings you closer together.

ENCOURAGE A FRIEND TODAY.

Send a card to your friend to show her you care.

Friends are gifts from God.

$\mathscr{Y}$our friend is the [person] who knows all about you and still likes you.

ELBERT HUBBARD

ENCOURAGE A FRIEND TODAY.

Compliment a friend's new outfit.

Sometimes friends just need a listening ear.

$\mathcal{A}$ loyal friend. . .sympathizes with
your problems when they're not so bad.

ARNOLD H. GLASGOW

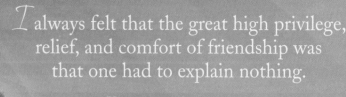

I always felt that the great high privilege, relief, and comfort of friendship was that one had to explain nothing.

KATHERINE MANSFIELD

Friends bring joy into our lives
like no one else can.

$\mathcal{A}$ man of many companions may come to ruin,
but there is a friend who sticks closer than a brother.

PROVERBS 18:24 NIV

ENCOURAGE A FRIEND TODAY.

Surprise your friend with
a bouquet of flowers.

Every gift from a friend is
a wish for your happiness.

RICHARD BACH

Friendship is a cozy shelter from life's rainy days.

UNKNOWN

Friendship is the hardest thing in the world to explain. It's not something you learn in school. But if you haven't learned the meaning of friendship, you really haven't learned anything.

MUHAMMAD ALI

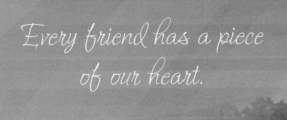

Every friend has a piece
of our heart.

No road is long with good company.

*T*rue friends will laugh at your jokes—
even if they aren't all that funny.

The better part of one's life
consists of his friendships.

ABRAHAM LINCOLN

Pray for your friends.

Friends know how to bring
out the best in us.

FUN WITH FRIENDS

Take photos during an outing with friends.
Then make a scrapbook collage to remember the day.

The language of friendship is not words but meanings.

HENRY DAVID THOREAU

True friends become
your extended family.

FUN WITH FRIENDS

Designate a weekly get-together with
your friends to watch a television
show or sporting event.

We don't laugh because we're happy—
we're happy because we laugh.

WILLIAM JAMES

Silence between friends will bring
you closer than a thousand words.

Good friends are good
for your health.

Irwin Sarason

The only way to have a
friend is to be one.

Ralph Waldo Emerson

There isn't any problem that can't be solved with laughter among friends.

*I*f one falls down, his friend can help him up. But pity the man who falls and has no one to help him up!

ECCLESIASTES 4:10 NIV

Friends are our comfort when we
need a shoulder to lean on.

Thank You, God, for my friends!

Friendship needs no words...

DAG HAMMARSKJOLD

Even something as simple as going to the mall with friends creates lifelong memories.

Always forgive your friends,
because we all make mistakes.

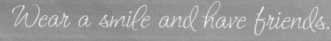

Wear a smile and have friends.

GEORGE ELIOT

*W*hen a friend is in trouble, don't annoy him
by asking if there is anything you can do.
Think up something appropriate and do it.

EDGAR WATSON HOWE

*I*f you truly love and enjoy your friends,
they are a part of the golden circle that makes life good.

MARJORIE HOLMES

God's love shines through our friends.

Friendship is a gift from God.

$\mathscr{A}$ friend is one who walks
in when others walk out.

WALTER WINCHELL

$\mathcal{F}$riends are people who help you up when you're down; and if they can't, they lie down beside you and listen.

UNKNOWN

*Friends are relatives
you make for yourself.*

EUSTACHE DESCHAMPS

Memories of our friends bring us joy.

ENCOURAGE A FRIEND

Surprise your friend with a homemade gift.

*L*et us be grateful to people who make us happy; they are the charming gardeners who make our souls blossom.

MARCEL PROUST

FUN WITH FRIENDS

Plan a mini getaway with your friends.

No matter our age, old friends can make us feel young again.

"Greater love has no one than this,
that he lay down his life for his friends."

John 15:13 NIV

You never know when God is introducing
you to a new friend. Be kind to everyone.

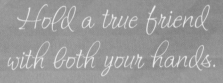

*Hold a true friend
with both your hands.*

NIGERIAN PROVERB

FUN WITH FRIENDS

Roll the windows down
and sing with your friends.

$\mathcal{F}$riendship is born at that moment when one person says to another, "What! You too? I thought I was the only one."

C. S. Lewis

*F*riends know all the inside jokes and
will still laugh about them years later.

Before you fall, a friend will already be there to catch you.

Friendship is built over time and shared memories.

$\mathcal{T}$ruly great friends are hard to find,
difficult to leave, and impossible to forget.

UNKNOWN

$\mathcal{N}$ever be too proud to ask your friends for help.
Their company will make a job more fun.

*W*hen it's dark and you're lost,
a friend will be there with a flashlight.

Live a life filled with love.

EPHESIANS 5:2 NLT

*T*rue friendship comes when the silence
between two people is comfortable.

DAVID TYSON GENTRY

The company of friends will warm your heart—
just like you've returned home.

Never forget to tell your friends how much they mean to you.

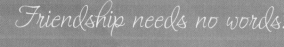

Friendship needs no words.

UNKNOWN

There is one friend in the life of each of us who seems not a separate person, however dear and beloved, but an expansion, an interpretation, of one's self, the very meaning of one's soul.

EDITH WHARTON

*I*f a friend confides in you,
always keep her secrets.

A friendly smile makes you happy.

Proverbs 15:30 CEV

If you ever feel lonely,
remember God is always with you.

Carry each other's burdens, and in this way
you will fulfill the law of Christ.

GALATIANS 6:2 NIV

*B*ring out the best in your friends,
and they'll bring out the best in you.

Friendship is the golden thread that ties the heart of the world.

JOHN EVELYN

ENCOURAGE A FRIEND

Send your friend a handwritten letter.

$\mathcal{N}$o argument is worth losing a friend.
Know when to agree to disagree.

You meet people who forget you. You forget people
you meet. But sometimes you meet those people
you can't forget. Those are your friends.

UNKNOWN

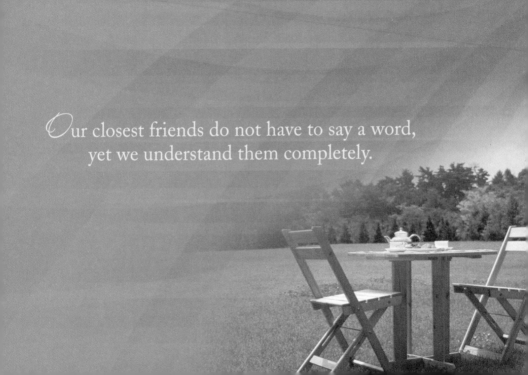

*O*ur closest friends do not have to say a word,
yet we understand them completely.

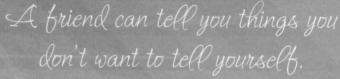

A friend can tell you things you don't want to tell yourself.

Frances Ward Weller

A friend allows you to be you—
and loves you for it.

*E*very friend changes our lives;
embrace the change and smile.

Fate chooses your relations;
you choose your friends.

JACQUES DELILLE

ENCOURAGE A FRIEND

Greet your friend with a giant hug.

If a friend hurts your feelings, be quick to forgive. If you hurt your friend's feelings, be quick to say, "I'm sorry."

Everyone hears what you say. Friends listen to what you say. Best friends listen to what you don't say.

UNKNOWN

Friends can be completely
honest with each other.

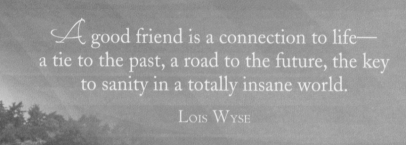

$\mathcal{A}$ good friend is a connection to life—
a tie to the past, a road to the future, the key
to sanity in a totally insane world.

Lois Wyse

$\mathcal{B}$lessed are they who have the gift of making friends,
for it is one of God's greatest gifts. It involves many
things, but above all the power of going out of one's self
and appreciating whatever is noble and loving in another.

THOMAS HUGHES

Best friends are soul mates.

Cry with a friend when she's sad—
then lift her up.

*E*ven if you completely embarrass yourself,
a friend will laugh and love you anyway.

Yesterday brought the beginning, tomorrow brings
the end, and somewhere in the middle
we became the best of friends.

Unknown

Confide in your friends.
They truly want the best for you.

The sweet smell of incense can make you feel good, but true friendship is better still.

PROVERBS 27:9 CEV

The oddest similarities can bring friends closer.

$\mathcal{F}$riends inspire us to dream and
live to our full potential.

You can make new friends every day,
if you give people a chance.

In my friend, I find a second self.

ISABEL NORTON

Friends make life worthwhile.

*Friendship needs to be cared for in order
to grow and bloom into its full beauty.*

Your friends will know you better in the first minute
you meet than your acquaintances
will know you in a thousand years.

RICHARD BACH

No matter how busy you are,
make time for your friends.

Friends should inspire one another.

*N*ever let jealousy interfere with your friendships; instead, love one another.

A friend is someone who knows the song
in your heart and can sing it back to you
when you have forgotten the words.

UNKNOWN

One loyal friend is worth
ten thousand relatives.

EURIPIDES

FUN WITH FRIENDS

Meet friends for coffee and conversation.

$\mathcal{A}$ friend is a gift you give yourself.

ROBERT LOUIS STEVENSON

$\mathcal{F}$riends may not recall all their fun times together,
but they remember the importance of their relationship.

Choose your friends wisely.

If you hurt a friend, be the first to say, "I'm sorry."

You can always tell a real friend: When you've
made a fool of yourself, he doesn't feel
you've done a permanent job.

LAURENCE J. PETER

$\mathcal{W}$hat sweetness is left in life if you take away friendship? It is like robbing the world of the sun.

MARCUS TULLIUS CICERO

ENCOURAGE A FRIEND

Reach out to friends in need before
they ask for your help.

Friendship consists of compromises.

If you ask for an honest opinion from your friends, accept it, even if the answer was not what you expected to hear.

Friends do not have to agree on everything.
They learn to accept each other as individuals.

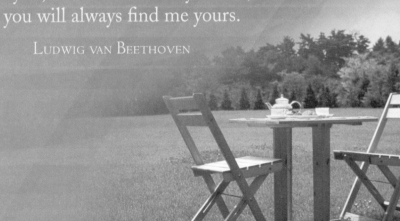

$\mathcal{N}$ever shall I forget the times I spent
with you; continue to be my friend,
as you will always find me yours.

LUDWIG VAN BEETHOVEN

A friend will change her plans
just to be with you.

The recipe for friendship is
laughter, love, and memories.

Communication is essential to friendship.

I want my friend to miss me
as long as I miss him.

St. Augustine

FUN WITH FRIENDS

Embark on an unexpected adventure with a friend.

$\mathcal{A}$ single rose can be my garden. . .
a single friend, my world.

LEO BUSCAGLIA

*W*hile friends come and go,
you'll never forget the times you shared.

Faithful friends will
stand up for one another.

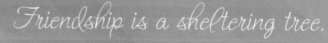

Friendship is a sheltering tree.

SAMUEL TAYLOR COLERIDGE

Be thankful for the friends you have.

$\mathcal{F}$riendship multiplies the good
of life and divides the evil.

BALTASAR GRACIAN

Loyalty and trust create unbreakable bonds between friends.

Happiness is a gift we give our friends.

$\mathcal{L}$ive life fully while you're here. Experience everything.
Take care of yourself and your friends.

ANTHONY ROBBINS

Stay in touch with friends,
no matter how many miles separate you.

Friendship is a beautiful ride.
Enjoy every second.

My best friend is the one who
brings out the best in me.

HENRY FORD

*E*ncourage your friends to fulfill
their wildest dreams.

True friends will laugh with you when you're happy
and cry with you when you're sad.

I thank my God every time I remember you.

PHILIPPIANS 1:3 NIV

Friends are a precious gift from God.

*I*t only takes a smile to brighten
a friend's gloomy day.

$\mathcal{L}$ots of people want to ride with you in the limo,
but what you want is someone who will take the
bus with you when the limo breaks down.

Oprah Winfrey

FUN WITH FRIENDS

Call a friend. Talk about your day.

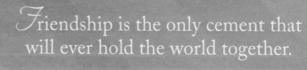

Friendship is the only cement that will ever hold the world together.

WOODROW WILSON

Support your friends' dreams,
and they'll reciprocate.

$\mathcal{D}$on't walk in front of me; I may not follow.
Don't walk behind me; I may not lead.
Just walk beside me and be my friend.

ALBERT CAMUS

ENCOURAGE A FRIEND

When you go on vacation,
surprise your friend with a postcard.

Let your best be for your friend.

KAHLIL GIBRAN

In the company of friends, even the dullest day
can bring lasting memories.

$\mathcal{T}$rue friends are always together in spirit.

L. M. MONTGOMERY

Friends will always be there
to wipe away your tears.

It's the friends you can call
up at 4 a.m. that matter.

MARLENE DIETRICH

Treat your friends the same way
you want to be treated.

*E*veryone has a gift for something,
even if it is the gift of being a good friend.

MARIAN ANDERSON

Learn to understand one another.

What starts as an acquaintance can bloom into a lifelong friendship.

FUN WITH FRIENDS

Deepen your friendships by scheduling a weekly event.
Watch a movie. Go to Bible study. Meet for coffee
and dessert. The possibilities are endless.

$\mathcal{A}$ faithful friend is the medicine of life.

APOCRYPHA

Friends can hold us together when
life becomes difficult.

True friends accept you
for who you are.

$\mathcal{A}$ friend is someone who understands
your past, believes in your future,
and accepts you just the way you are.

UNKNOWN

*O*ne shared smile may be the
beginning of a lasting friendship.

Small favors go a long way.

*E*very friend is different.
Learn to understand each other's needs.

*Friendship doubles your joys
and divides your sorrows.*

UNKNOWN

$\mathcal{D}$on't be dismayed at good-byes.
A farewell is necessary before you can meet again.
And meeting again, after moments or lifetimes,
is certain for those who are friends.

RICHARD BACH

Be patient with your friends.

FUN WITH FRIENDS

Participate in a new activity with a friend—
rollerblading, jogging, white-water rafting. . .
It's not so scary when you share
new adventures with your friends.

$\mathcal{T}$here is nothing better than
the encouragement of a good friend.

KATHARINE BUTLER HATHAWAY

True friends walk hand in hand,
guiding each other to greatness.

$\mathcal{A}$ friend is one of the nicest things you can have, and one of the best things you can be.

DOUGLAS PAGELS

True friends help each other
grow into better people.

*H*elp your friends—even when
it's not convenient for you.

*W*hen we seek to discover the best in others,
we somehow bring out the best in ourselves.

WILLIAM ARTHUR WARD

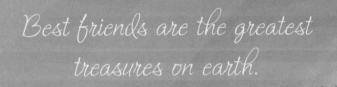

Best friends are the greatest
treasures on earth.

Friends accept each other's faults.

I cannot even imagine where I would be today were it not for that handful of friends who have given me a heart full of joy. Let's face it, friends make life a lot more fun.

CHARLES R. SWINDOLL

True friendship is based on trust.

Don't sweat the small stuff.
Friends don't have to agree on everything.

Never take your friends for granted.

*W*alking with a friend in the dark is
better than walking alone in the light.

HELEN KELLER

Make a friend laugh when she's upset.
She'll love you for it.

Love is blind, but friendship closes its eyes.

UNKNOWN

*A faithful friend is
an image of God.*

FRENCH PROVERB

$\mathscr{H}$appiness is time spent with a friend and
looking forward to sharing time with [her] again.

Lee Wilkinson